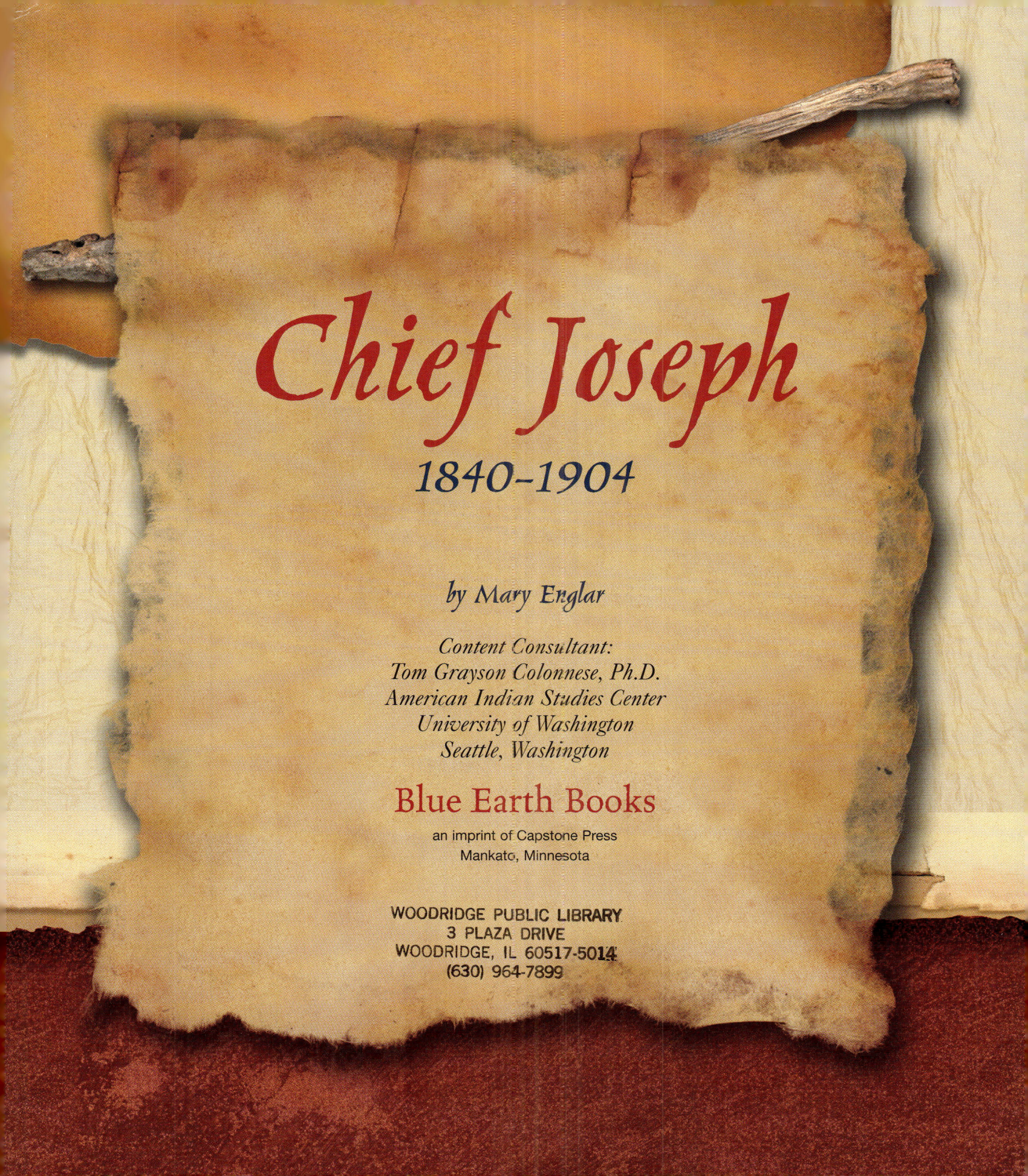

Chief Joseph

1840–1904

by Mary Englar

Content Consultant:
Tom Grayson Colonnese, Ph.D.
American Indian Studies Center
University of Washington
Seattle, Washington

Blue Earth Books

an imprint of Capstone Press
Mankato, Minnesota

Blue Earth Books are published by Capstone Press
151 Good Counsel Drive, P.O. Box 669, Mankato, Minnesota 56002
http://www.capstonepress.com

Library of Congress Cataloging-in-Publication Data
Englar, Mary.
    Chief Joseph, 1840–1904 / by Mary Englar.
       p. cm—(American Indian biographies)
    Summary: A biography of the peace chief who ended the Nez Perce war by surrendering to United
States soldiers in 1877, believing that he would be permitted to lead his people back to their ancestral lands in
Idaho. Includes a recipe for berry fritters and directions for "the stick game."
    Includes bibliographical references and index.
    ISBN 0-7368-2444-8 (hardcover)
    1. Joseph, Nez Perce chief, 1840–1904—Juvenile literature. 2. Nez Perce Indians—Kings and rulers
Biography—Juvenile literature. 3. Nez Perce Indians—Wars, 1877—Juvenile literature. [1. Joseph, Nez Perce
chief, 1840–1904. 2. Nez Perce Indians—Biography. 3. Indians of North America—Northwest, Pacific—
Biography. 4. Kings, queens, rulers, etc.] I. Title. II. Series.
E99.N5J5824 2004
979.5004'9741—dc21   2003011071

Editorial Credits

Editor: Christine Peterson
Series Designers: Jennifer Bergstrom and
    Heather Kindseth
Book Designer: Jennifer Bergstrom
Photo Researcher: Wanda Winch
Product Planning Editor: Eric Kudalis

1 2 3 4 5 6 09 08 07 06 05 04

Photo Credits

Cover images: Marilyn "Angel" Wynn, eagle
feather; Tongel Art Studio/Jayme Van Tongel,
Chief Joseph

Capstone Press/Gary Sundermeyer, 11, 27;
Corbis/Christie's Images, 24; Corbis/Kit
Houghton, 15; Corbis/Michael S. Louis, 21;
Courtesy of Frederic Remington Art Museum,
Ogdensburg, New York, 6; Courtesy of Mrs. John
Clymer and the Clymer Museum of Art, 18; David
Jensen, 8–9; Denver Public Library, 5; Getty
Images/Hulton Archive, 17; Idaho State Historical
Society, 13; Montana Historical Society, Helena, 4,
29 (top); MSCUA, University of Washington
Libraries, 14, 16, 26, 28; North Wind Picture
Archives, 12, 20; The Greenwich Workshop
Inc./Howard Terpning, 23, 29 (bottom)

Contents

"I Will Fight No More Forever"

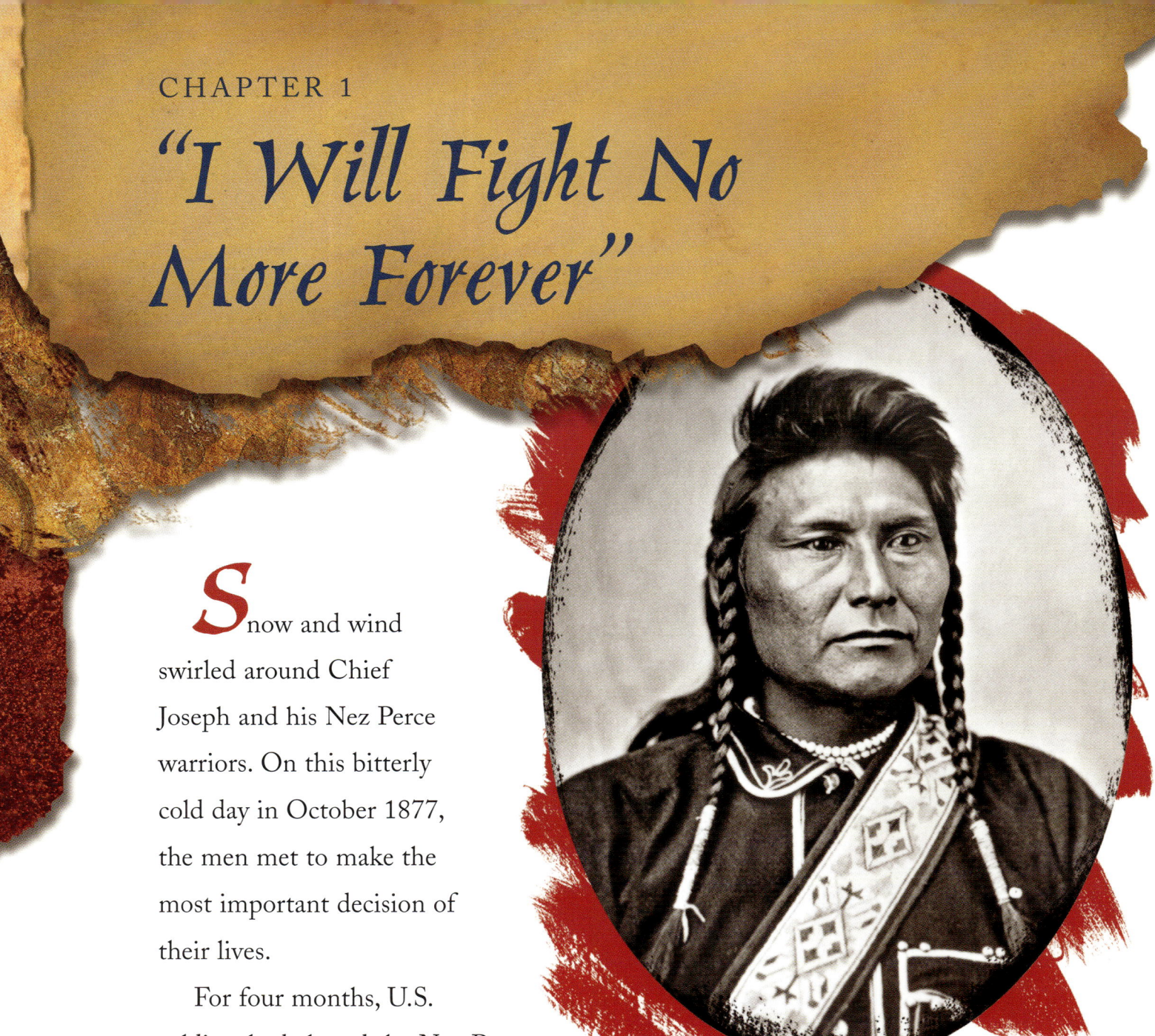

Snow and wind swirled around Chief Joseph and his Nez Perce warriors. On this bitterly cold day in October 1877, the men met to make the most important decision of their lives.

For four months, U.S. soldiers had chased the Nez Perce. Joseph and 750 Nez Perce men, women, and children had traveled over rugged mountains. They carried their belongings and pushed their herds of

▲ *Chief Joseph helped lead the Nez Perce as they fled from U.S. soldiers. The Nez Perce chief was photographed in 1877.*

▲ *U.S. soldiers launched a surprise attack against the Nez Perce camp in 1877. This picture of the attack is based on a drawing done by G. M. Holland. Holland's drawing was printed in* Harper's Weekly *on November 3, 1877.*

livestock through narrow trails. Now, only 40 miles (64 kilometers) from the Canadian border, the Nez Perce were trapped.

Joseph heard his people crying from hunger and grief. He saw women and children hiding in holes to escape gunfire. Many Nez Perce had been killed during the months of fighting, including Joseph's brother Ollokot.

The soldiers told Joseph that the Nez Perce could return to their land in Idaho if they **surrendered**. But the warriors did not trust the soldiers. The warriors wanted to keep moving. Joseph knew his people could escape if they left the sick and wounded behind. But he refused to leave his people.

Joseph had made his decision. He picked up his rifle. Joseph and a few warriors left the camp. Bullets had torn holes in Joseph's sleeves and pants. Scars marked his forehead. Joseph approached the soldiers. He quietly laid down his rifle.

▲ *Heavy fighting between the Nez Perce and U.S. soldiers resulted in Chief Joseph's surrender. Western artist Frederic Remington painted this version of Chief Joseph's surrender in the late 1880s.*

Joseph told the soldiers he was tired of fighting. Many of his people were wounded or dead. He said, "Hear me, my chiefs! I am tired. My heart is sick and sad. From where the sun now stands, I will fight no more forever."

The Nez Perce War ended with the surrender of Chief Joseph. At least 120 Nez Perce men, women, and children were killed during the war. Their journey covered a staggering trail of 1,170 miles (1,883 kilometers).

Chief Joseph said that given the chance, people of every color would "be all alike—brothers of one father and one mother, with one sky above us and one country around us and one government for all."

When he surrendered, Joseph was tired, worn, and far from home. He longed to return to where his life began in the Wallowa Valley of Oregon.

Battle at
Bear Paw

BEARPAW
MOUNTAINS

Battle at
Big Hole

BITTERROOT RANGE

Wallowa
Valley

Salmon River

Snake River

Legend

✷ Battle

⛰ Mountain Range

⌇ Nez Perce Route
Toward Canada

▮ 1855 Reservation

▯ 1863 Reservation

⌇ River

〶 Valley

Miles
0   50   100   150   200
0   50   100   150   200
Kilometers

United
States

N
W   E
S

CHAPTER 2

Life in the Wallowa Valley

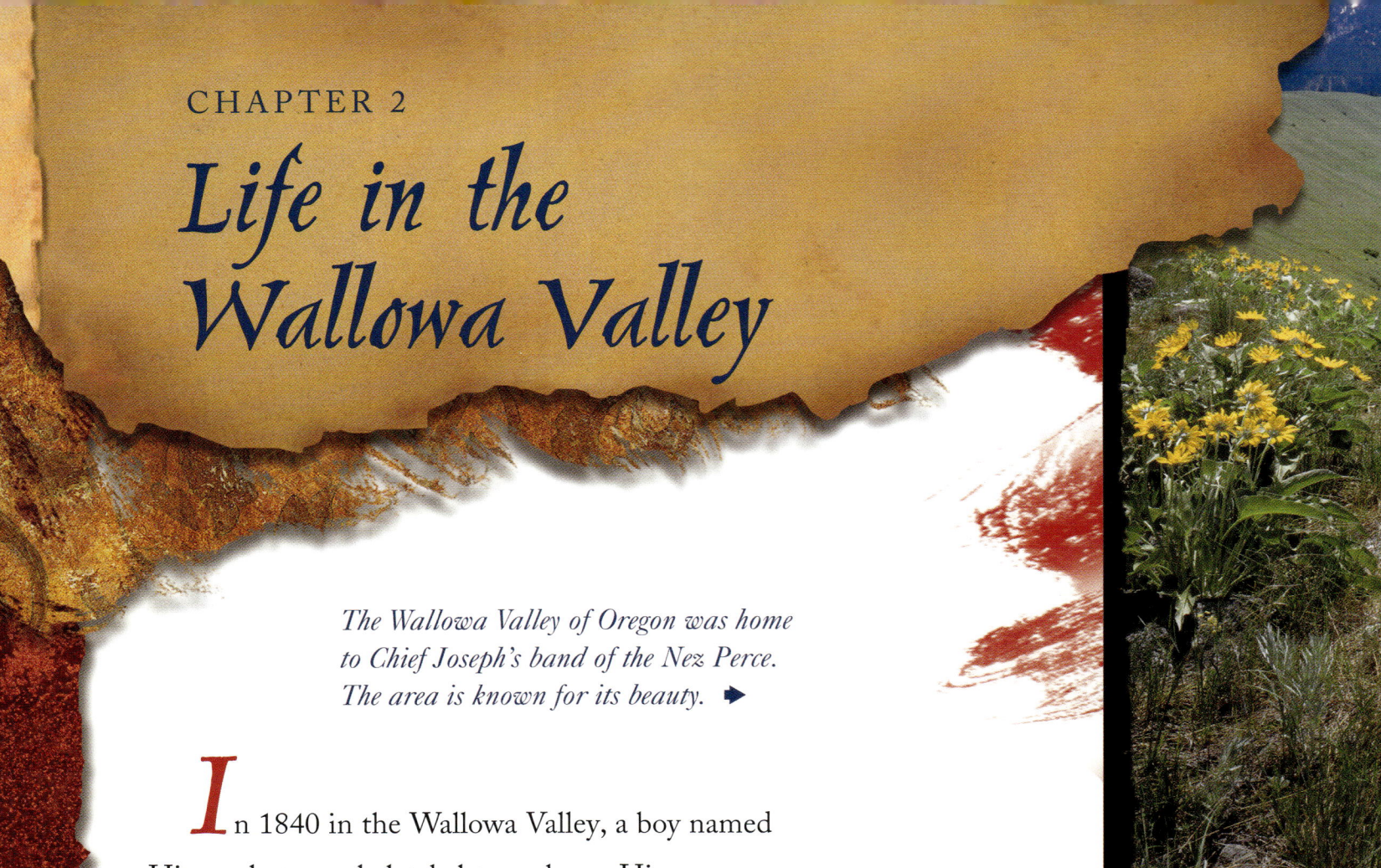

The Wallowa Valley of Oregon was home to Chief Joseph's band of the Nez Perce. The area is known for its beauty. ➤

In 1840 in the Wallowa Valley, a boy named Hin-mah-too-yah-lat-keht was born. His name means Thunder Traveling to High Mountains. **Missionaries** later **baptized** the boy and named him Joseph. Joseph's people had lived in the Wallowa Valley as long as they could remember. The boy's father, Tuekakas, was the peace chief of his **band**. Joseph's mother, Khapkhaponimi, and Tuekakas had seven children.

When Joseph was a child, his family lived like the Nez Perce had for hundreds of years. They hunted elk, deer, and bighorn sheep that grazed on the thick grasses in the Wallowa Valley. Joseph's band kept large herds of horses that roamed through the valley. In spring, the Nez Perce caught salmon in the nearby rivers. The valley supplied nearly everything they needed.

In winter, Joseph's family moved into nearby canyons. The deep canyons protected their village from the strong winter winds that blew on the high, flat **plateaus**.

The people built **lodges** that looked much like tepees. The walls were covered with mats, which the women wove from tall grasses. Sometimes, a village built a longhouse that sheltered many families.

When spring came, Joseph's family packed their horses and moved to summer camps. The Nez Perce moved around to find fresh food for themselves and grass for their horses.

"I have carried a heavy load on my back ever since I was a boy. I learned then that we were but few, while the white men were many, and that we could not hold our own with them. We were like deer. They were like grizzly bears."

—Chief Joseph

That All People May Be One,
published quotes from an 1879 interview for North American Review

In spring, salmon came up the rivers from the Pacific Ocean. In the Nez Perce **tribe**, catching fish was the men's job. Joseph helped the men and boys build platforms out into the rivers. There, they speared, netted, and trapped hundreds of salmon.

The mountain meadows and hillsides also provided food for the Nez Perce. Women dug up carrots, onions, and other wild roots. Women and children picked blackberries, strawberries, and huckleberries.

Joseph's people were friendly with most of the neighboring tribes. They traded with the Flathead Indians in Montana. Every year, Joseph's family brought dried fish, berries, bows, and arrows to trade with the Flathead Indians. In return, the Nez Perce received buffalo robes, beads, feathers, and pipes. The Nez Perce also traded with tribes in western Oregon. Joseph's people brought horses, dried meat, and animal hides. In return, they received fish oil, baskets, and ocean shells.

As peace chief, Joseph's father, Tuekakas, cared for the needs of his people. From a young age, Joseph watched as his father solved problems for the people of their village. Tuekakas was known as a calm, peaceful man. He taught Joseph to respect and love all living things.

Berry Fritters

Berries were an important food for the Nez Perce. In summer, they climbed to mountain meadows and collected many kinds of berries. The sweet fruit was a treat. They dried the berries and used them to flavor their food in the winter. Blueberries or huckleberries can be used in this traditional recipe.

What You Need

Ingredients

2 cups (480 mL) blueberries or huckleberries

3 cups (720 mL) unbleached flour

½ cup (120 mL) sugar

1¼ teaspoons (6.2 mL) baking powder

½ cup (120 mL) water

3 eggs

6 cups (1.5 L) vegetable oil for frying

Equipment

large mixing bowl

dry-ingredient measuring cups

measuring spoons

mixing spoons

small mixing bowl

liquid measuring cup

wire whisk

heavy saucepan

tablespoon

metal slotted spoon

plate

paper towels

What You Do

1. Rinse berries and set them aside to dry.
2. In a large mixing bowl, mix together the flour, sugar, and baking powder.
3. In a small mixing bowl, use a wire whisk to beat water and eggs until foamy.
4. Pour egg mixture into the dry ingredients and use a mixing spoon to combine the ingredients.
5. Stir in berries.
6. Heat oil in a heavy saucepan to 350°F (180°C) or until a cube of bread turns golden brown after cooking 1 minute.
7. Drop mixture by tablespoons into the hot oil. Let the fritters cook for 5 to 10 minutes or until one side is golden brown.
8. Use a metal slotted spoon to turn fritters over and cook for another 5 to 10 minutes.
9. With the metal slotted spoon, remove fritter from the oil and drain fritters on a plate covered with paper towels.
10. Serve hot.
11. Serve with extra berries, if desired.

Makes 2 dozen fritters

CHAPTER 3

The White Men Come

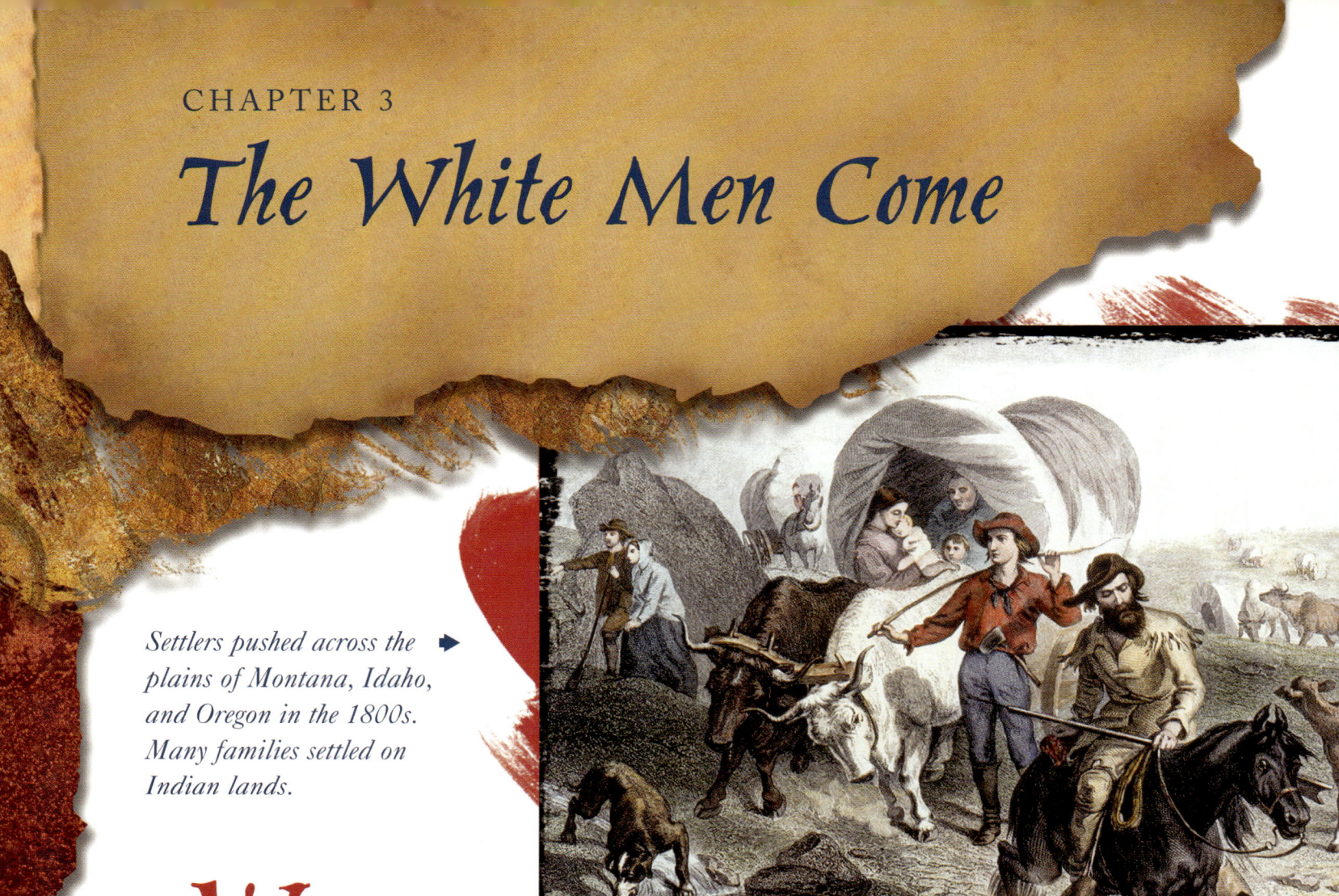

Settlers pushed across the plains of Montana, Idaho, and Oregon in the 1800s. Many families settled on Indian lands.

When Joseph was a boy, thousands of settlers traveled to the Oregon Territory. Most settlers followed the Oregon Trail, which passed south of the valley where Joseph lived. High mountains and deep river canyons protected the Wallowa Valley from the settlers. Tuekakas warned his people to stay away from the settlers and their military forts.

Joseph and his father heard many stories about American Indians who had lost their land. Tuekakas feared that his band might lose its land too. Joseph's father knew they could never fight such a large group of soldiers and settlers and win.

In 1855, representatives of the U.S. government asked members of all Indian tribes in the Northwest to attend a **council**. About 2,500 Nez Perce came to the Walla Walla Valley in present-day Washington to meet with government leaders.

Tuekakas brought Joseph along. Joseph was only 15. He stayed at the camp and took care of the horses. In the evening, Joseph listened as his father and other Nez Perce chiefs talked about the council.

The government wanted to buy the Indians' land. In return, the Indians would receive about $200,000 from the government over six years. Government leaders said the Indians could hunt and fish on the new **reservation**. They also promised the Indians houses, land, and schools.

The Wallowa Valley was part of the new Nez Perce Reservation. Tuekakas signed the **treaty**. Joseph's

▲ *Nez Perce warriors, like the ones pictured above, would often wear headdresses and carry war poles when they met with soldiers or people from other tribes.*

father believed that the treaty gave his people the Wallowa Valley forever.

After the Treaty of 1855, many tribes refused to leave their homelands and move to the reservations. Other tribes went to war against the settlers and the U.S. Army.

The Nez Perce did not join the fight. But their peaceful times ended in the 1860s when settlers found gold on the Nez Perce Reservation. Once again, the U.S. government called for a council. At least 3,000 Nez Perce met with government leaders at Lapwai on the Nez Perce Reservation.

The government wanted all the Nez Perce to move to a much smaller reservation in what is now Idaho. The government wanted to take nearly 7 million acres (2.8 million hectares) of Nez Perce land, including the Wallowa Valley.

Many chiefs, including Tuekakas, became angry at the news of a new treaty. They said the Treaty of 1855 gave them their land forever. Tuekakas and other chiefs refused to sign the Treaty of 1863 and left the council.

When Joseph and his father returned to the Wallowa Valley, they built a fence at the mouth of the valley. The fence was a warning to settlers to stay out of the Wallowa Valley. Tuekakas was angry, but he told Joseph not to fight the white men. There were too many of them.

▼ *In 1855, the Nez Perce camped outside Old Fort Walla Walla. Talks between the U.S. leaders and the Nez Perce lasted several days.*

Nez Perce and the Appaloosas

By the end of the 1700s, the Nez Perce owned some of the largest herds of Appaloosas in North America. In the 1600s, Spanish explorers first introduced the spotted horse to the Americas. The Nez Perce began raising and using Appaloosas in the early 1700s. The Nez Perce had at least 10,000 horses roaming the northwestern United States.

The Nez Perce carefully bred their horses for speed and strength. They wanted their horses to be swift in battle and strong like workhorses. The Nez Perce needed horses to carry large amounts of buffalo meat back from the Great Plains. The horses also helped people travel faster and farther when they were hunting or trading goods. Horse racing was a favorite activity when Nez Perce bands came together.

When the Nez Perce War ended, soldiers captured or killed many of the Nez Perce's horses. Some Appaloosas were sold to settlers and bred with other horses. Many of the original Appaloosas survived and were saved by ranchers in Idaho. In 1938, the Appaloosa Horse Club was formed to restore the original strength and beauty of the Appaloosa. The Nez Perce still raise Appaloosas in Idaho.

◀ *Appaloosas are known for their strength and speed.*

15

CHAPTER 4

Joseph Becomes Chief

Chief Joseph became peace chief after his father's death. Joseph, pictured here in 1903, was a leader for his people throughout his life. ➤

As Tuekakas got older, he found it harder to lead his people. He was going blind and becoming very weak. Joseph slowly began to take over his father's duties. Joseph was very much like his father. He was tall and strong, but he had a gentle way about him. He spoke well, and the Nez Perce saw him as a wise leader. Joseph knew that some settlers were grazing their herds of horses and cattle in the valley. Settlers were going against laws set up by the Treaty of 1855. Still, Joseph believed the Nez Perce and settlers could live together peacefully.

By 1871, Tuekakas was very sick. He called his son to him before he died. Joseph promised to never give up their land. The Wallowa Valley held the bones of their ancestors and soon would hold Tuekakas' grave too. When his father died, Joseph buried him in the land his father loved best.

In January 1877, U.S. government leaders ordered all the Nez Perce to move onto the new reservation by April. Joseph refused to move. Joseph and other Nez Perce chiefs agreed to meet with military leaders. Joseph wanted the soldiers to know the truth. His father never signed the treaty giving up the Wallowa Valley.

At the meeting, many Nez Perce told General Oliver O. Howard that they never signed the Treaty of 1863. Howard said that another Nez Perce chief had signed the treaty for all of them. Toohoolhoolzote, an old chief, told Howard that the Nez Perce were free men. They would not give up their land. The chief's words made Howard angry. He ordered his guards to put the old chief in jail.

▲ *General Oliver O. Howard led the U.S. Army during the Nez Perce War. This engraving of Howard was done in 1870.*

▲ *The Nez Perce were forced to quickly pack their camps and move to a reservation. On the way, the Nez Perce fought with settlers. The U.S. Army then sent soldiers after the Nez Perce. The Nez Perce decided not to move to the reservation. They headed toward Canada as shown in this painting by John Clymer.*

The young Nez Perce were furious. They believed that Howard did not respect them or their chiefs. Howard ordered Joseph and the other chiefs to move to the reservation. If they did not, Howard said he would send soldiers to force them.

Joseph and the others felt trapped. They knew that if they did not agree,

it would mean war. Joseph knew the Nez Perce could not win a war against the U.S. Army. The Nez Perce finally agreed to move to the reservation. Howard then released the old chief from jail.

In May 1877, Howard gave the Nez Perce just 30 days to move to the reservation. Joseph said they needed more time for people to pack up their lodges and gather their animals. Joseph said the Snake River and Salmon River were too high for his people to cross safely. But Howard did not change his mind. He told the Nez Perce to move to the reservation in one month or face war.

Joseph returned to his village. The band's horses and cattle were running free in the Wallowa Valley. As quickly as possible, Joseph and his band prepared to move. The young men rounded up as many horses and cattle as they could find. The women took down the lodges and collected extra food. As they started down the trail to Lapwai, many Nez Perce believed they would never see the Wallowa Valley again.

Joseph led his band to camas fields near Tolo Lake in present-day Idaho. These fields filled with the cama flowers were a favorite meeting place for Joseph's people. They camped there with other Nez Perce bands. Women dug camas bulbs and dried them in the sun. They mashed the bulbs into flour. The men fished and hunted. It reminded Joseph of how good life once was for his people.

But life at Tolo Lake was far from peaceful. Chiefs from the different bands talked about their loss of freedom. Young men raced through the camp and fired their guns in the air. Joseph worried that they were thinking about war. All their sadness over losing their land had turned to anger.

While Joseph was away, several young men rode out of camp and killed settlers who were living on Nez Perce land. The warriors believed the settlers had killed members of the Nez Perce tribe. After hearing about the deaths, the U.S. Army sent soldiers to capture the Nez Perce.

CHAPTER 5

The Nez Perce War

Fighting began between the Nez Perce and U.S. soldiers in 1877. The two sides fought many battles as the Nez Perce traveled across Idaho and Montana. ➤

Joseph had never wanted war, but war came to him. Joseph tried to keep the Nez Perce from fighting, but the other chiefs wanted war. The Nez Perce and soldiers fought many battles. But the Nez Perce managed to escape.

In June 1877, war chiefs decided that the Nez Perce should go to Montana. Every day, Joseph and his people got farther away from their home. The Nez Perce pushed east, where they faced the rugged trails of the Bitterroot Range. About 750

▲ *A memorial now marks the site of the Battle at Big Hole. Each feather stands for a Nez Perce man, woman, or child killed during the battle.*

people and 2,000 horses climbed over a narrow trail. For nine days, they struggled up to the top of the mountains and then down into the Bitterroot Valley of Montana. Two weeks later, General Howard and his soldiers climbed the trail behind them.

Once they crossed into Montana, Joseph and the other chiefs believed the Nez Perce were safe. They did not believe soldiers would follow them across the rough mountain trail.

On August 7, 1877, the Nez Perce stopped near the Big Hole River. Some chiefs decided it was a safe place to camp. They set up new lodges. Men went hunting. For the first time in months, the Nez Perce felt safe.

Early the next morning, Joseph woke to the sound of gunfire. Soldiers had launched a surprise attack. Women and children screamed as bullets tore into the lodges. Warriors scrambled to find their weapons and defend their people.

Joseph's first thoughts were of his people. The people in the camp were injured and confused. He told the women to pack up the horses. Joseph led his people away from the battle.

The warriors continued to fight the soldiers into the night. The next morning, the warriors left the battlefield and rode to catch up with their families. At least 60 Nez Perce died in the Battle at Big Hole, most of them women and children.

For the next month, the Nez Perce fled from the soldiers. Many people were sick. Joseph worried that they would run out of food before winter.

Some chiefs said they should try to reach Canada. Others feared more people would get sick if they did not stop to rest and hunt for food. When they came to the Bearpaw Mountains in northern Montana, the chiefs decided to stop. The people rested and ate fresh buffalo meat for the first time in weeks.

The next morning, a Nez Perce scout rode swiftly into the camp. The scout had seen large clouds of dust from running buffalo. He thought soldiers had scared the buffalo. Some families immediately caught their horses and began to take down their lodges. Others were not afraid and continued to eat breakfast. Children played in the mud along the creek. Less than an hour later, word came that at least 100 U.S. soldiers were charging toward the camp.

Suddenly, everyone hurried to catch the horses and get away. Warriors grabbed their rifles and

▲ *Joseph and a small group of Nez Perce warriors traveled across snow-covered land to meet U.S. soldiers to surrender, as shown in this 1982 painting by Howard Terpning.*

climbed the hills above the camp. Joseph rushed women and children into hiding places. He then joined the warriors to defend the camp.

Soldiers soon surrounded the camp. Joseph realized they were trapped. For five days, Joseph watched as more warriors were killed, including his brother Ollokot. Joseph knew his people had few choices.

On October 5, 1877, Chief Joseph surrendered to the soldiers. After so many months and so many deaths, the Nez Perce War was over.

CHAPTER 6

Life after the War

After the war, Chief Joseph continued his fight to return to the Wallowa Valley in Oregon. He posed for this portrait in 1903. ➤

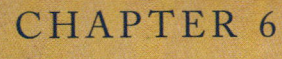

After he surrendered, soldiers promised Joseph his people would be able to return to Idaho in the spring. Joseph believed the soldiers.

The soldiers did not keep their promise. Joseph and his band were sent first to Kansas and then to Oklahoma. The Nez Perce were not used to Oklahoma's hot, steamy summers. They had no horses or guns to go hunting. They found it difficult to raise crops in the unfamiliar soil. Many Nez Perce were sick

"Tell General Howard I know his heart. What he told me before, I have it in my heart. I am tired of fighting. Our chiefs are killed. Looking Glass is dead. Toohoolhoolzote is dead. The old men are all dead. It is the young men who say, 'Yes' or 'No.' He who led the young men is dead. It is cold, and we have no blankets. The little children are freezing to death. My people, some of them, have run away to the hills, and have no blankets, no food. No one knows where they are—perhaps freezing to death. I want to have time to look for my children, and see how many of them I can find. Maybe I shall find them among the dead. Hear me, my chiefs. I am tired. My heart is sick and sad. From where the sun now stands I will fight no more forever."

—Chief Joseph

Surrender speech as recorded in 1877 by Lieutenant C.E.S. Wood.

and dying in the strange southern land. They wanted to go home.

Joseph wrote a letter to the U. S. Army. He asked permission to go back to Idaho. The army refused.

Joseph would not give up. In 1879, he traveled to Washington, D.C., to meet with President Rutherford B. Hayes and other leaders. Joseph told them that his people were peaceful. He again asked that his people be sent back to the reservation in Idaho.

Many Americans knew about Chief Joseph from the newspapers. They began to write letters to the newspapers and to the government asking that Joseph be allowed to return home.

▲ *In 1884, Chief Joseph moved to the Colville Indian Reservation in Washington.*
His campsite was photographed in 1901 by Dr. Edward H. Latham.

In 1884, the U.S. government agreed to let some Nez Perce return to the reservation in Idaho. But Joseph could not return to Idaho. Settlers there were still afraid of him. Joseph and his band were sent to the Colville Reservation in what is now Washington state.

For most Nez Perce, the move to Colville ended the long and tragic journey they began seven years earlier. In Colville, the Nez Perce gradually settled back into their daily lives. They began to raise horses and cattle. They built new lodges. They hunted and fished. Joseph believed his journey was not over. He hoped that one day he would again live in the Wallowa Valley.

The Stick Game

The Nez Perce have played the stick game for hundreds of years. People of all ages enjoy playing this game. Teams sing or hum loudly to distract the other team. Some players beat on drums. A stick game will sometimes last for hours.

What You Need
11 craft sticks. One stick should be
longer than the other 10.
Paint
Paintbrushes
String or yarn
2 wooden spools or small pieces of wood

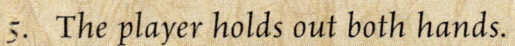

What You Do
1. Paint the craft sticks. Sticks can be painted differently for each team.
2. Tie a piece of string or yarn around one of the small wood pieces.

How to Play
1. Divide players into two teams. Each team gets five sticks.
2. Teams sit in a line facing each other.
3. A player from one team puts one of the small pieces of wood in each hand.
4. The player puts his or her hands behind his or her back and shuffles the pieces back and forth.

5. The player holds out both hands.
6. A player on the second team tries to guess which hand holds the wood piece marked with string. If the player guesses correctly, the second team wins a stick from the first team. If the second team guesses incorrectly, then the first team wins a stick.
7. A player on the second team now hides the wood pieces.
8. The game continues until one team wins all 10 sticks and the larger stick.

In 1905, Nez Perce leaders, Indians, and other officials gathered for a ceremony at Joseph's gravesite to honor the famous chief.

He led his people
in the Nez Perce War
of 1877.
Died Sept. 21, 1904.
Aged
about 60 years.

At Colville, Joseph continued to be a strong leader for his people. He traveled the country, speaking out about the Nez Perce and the broken treaties.

As the years passed, Joseph realized he would never return to his beloved homeland. He was growing old. On September 21, 1904, Joseph died as he sat by a fire outside his tepee. A doctor on the reservation said Joseph died of a broken heart. The great Nez Perce leader never returned to his home in the Wallowa Valley.

Chronology

1871

Tuekakas dies, and Joseph becomes peace chief.

1855

The Treaty of 1855 creates the first Nez Perce Reservation. The treaty includes the Wallowa Valley.

1904

Joseph dies on the Colville Reservation in Washington.

June 1877

War breaks out. Joseph and his band flee to Montana.

1840

Young Joseph is born in Wallowa Valley in what is today Oregon.

May 1877

Joseph's band is ordered to move to a new reservation in Idaho.

October 1877

Joseph surrenders his band to the U.S. Army.

1863

A second treaty reduces the Nez Perce Reservation by 90 percent; Joseph's band does not sign the treaty.

Glossary

band (BAND)—a group of Indian people who are related to each other; a band is smaller than a tribe.

baptize (BAP-tize)—to bring someone into the Christian religion

council (KOUN-suhl)—a meeting between American Indian leaders or between the leaders and the U.S. government representatives

lodge (LODJ)—a small house, cottage, or cabin; the Nez Perce lived in lodges made from woven mats.

missionary (MISH-uh-ner-ee)—a person sent by a church or religious group to teach that group's religion

plateau (pla-TOH)—a raised area of flat land

reservation (rez-ur-VAY-shun)—an area of land set aside for American Indians by the U.S. government

surrender (suh-REN-dur)—to give up in a fight or a battle

treaty (TREE-tee)—a legal agreement between nations

tribe (TRIBE)—a group of people who live in the same area, speak the same language, and obey the same chief

Read More

Klingel, Cynthia and Robert B. Noyed. *Chief Joseph: Chief of the Nez Perce.* Our People. Chanhassen, Minn.: Child's World, 2003.

Lassieur, Allison. *The Nez Perce Tribe.* Native Peoples. Mankato, Minn.: Bridgestone Books, 2000.

McLeese, Don. *Chief Joseph.* Native American Legends. Vero Beach, Fla.: Rourke, 2003.

Stout, Mary. *Nez Perce.* Native American Peoples. Milwaukee: Gareth Stevens, 2003.

Internet Sites

FactHound offers a safe, fun way to find Internet sites related to this book. All of the sites on FactHound have been researched by our staff.

Here's how:

1. Visit *www.facthound.com*
2. Type in this special code **0736824448** for age-appropriate sites. Or enter a search word related to this book for a more general search.
3. Click on the Fetch It button.

Facthound will fetch the best sites for you!

Useful Addresses

Big Hole National Battlefield
P.O. Box 237
Wisdom, MT 59761

Nez Perce National Historical Park
39063 U.S. Highway 95
Spalding, ID 83540-9715

Nez Perce Tribe
P.O. Box 365
Lapwai, ID 83540

Nez Perce National Historic Trail
12730 Highway 12
Orofino, ID 83544

Index